Call and Answer

Poems by Joyce Brown

Illustrated by Mary Swann

Call and Answer

The following poems have appeared in these journals:
     Yankee: "Power"
     Light: "Apple Pie"
     Smartish Pace: "Urgency of Birds"

Requests for information should be addressed to

 BrickHouse Books, Inc.
306 Suffolk Road
Baltimore, Maryland 21218 USA

ISBN-13: 978-0-932616-77-1
ISBN-10: 0-932616-77-1

Printed in the United States of America

Book Design:
Carmen M. Walsh
www.walshwriting.com

The Poet

Joyce S. Brown is a poet who lives in Baltimore, Maryland. Her poems have appeared in *Poetry, Smartish Pace, The American Scholar, The Christian Science Monitor, The Journal of Medical Humanities, Commonweal, Yankee, The Tennessee Quarterly,* and other journals. For 10 years, she was a teacher of high school English and world religions; for another 10, she taught fiction and poetry writing at Johns Hopkins University. She also served as poetry editor of Baltimore's *City Paper.* In retirement, she has tutored at a juvenile prison and is currently working with at-risk teens in a program called Learning Inc.

The Artist

Mary Swann is a landscape painter and quiltmaker who lives in New Park, Pennsylvania. A graduate of the Maryland Institute College of Art, she paints in Pennsylvania, Maryland, and Nova Scotia. For many years, as a member of the former Gomez and Paper Rock Scissors galleries, she showed her work regularly in Baltimore as well as in juried exhibitions throughout the USA. Her paintings are held in private collections both here and abroad, and one of her prints is owned by the Baltimore Museum of Art. Her monoprints also illustrate a children's book, *The Story of the Close Cat.*

Artist's Note

The poems chosen for *Call and Answer* from the large and varied body of Joyce's work were the ones that presented themselves to me in pictures. As it turns out, many of them are little dramas. It seems natural that a painter of scenes would feel most competent to respond to these.

The illustrations are not meant to demonstrate or explain the action taking place in the poems, but rather to provide a pictorial response to what is being expressed. I hope that they have managed to do some justice to the wit, awe, irony, and concern that inform the peculiar insight of these poems.

The spontaneous medium of monoprint seemed most appropriate to reflect the immediacy and truth of Joyce's thought.

—*Mary Swann*

Poet's Note

Mary's illustrations—playful, fresh, surprising—never betray the labor expended in the complicated printmaking process, and remind me of what Yeats wrote about poetry:

> *A line will take us hours maybe;*
> *Yet if it does not seem a moment's thought,*
> *Our stitching and unstitching has been naught.*

Each of Mary's responses delights me with its angle into the poem and the color, in every sense of that word, she gives to my words.

—*Joyce Brown*

for
Anne and Max

Contents

Empty Slate

"They're the luckiest who know they're not unique."
— Adrienne Rich

I like to think my mind's as great as Plato's—
maybe greater if it got in gear.
After all, I know much more
about this stony sphere
and what's beyond
than any of those Greeks
who took so long to count a horse's teeth.

I resolve while weeding pachysandra
to prove or disprove evolution,
to psychoanalyse Herr Freud,
to determine the degree of psyche
in the soma, to settle questions on heredity.

But nothing comes to me among the weeds
except the plans for dinner and the day.
While putting trowel and gloves away,
I wish for dream professors in the night,
courses sure to counsel me to light.

My morning mind's an empty slate.
There was no evening class in session,
and I have spent the darkened hours
in an unfamiliar parlor,
rearranging day-old flowers.

Umbrella of the Lake

When the beach umbrella flew up,
brisked by the wind, then tipped
to float boatlike on the lake,
the old man, fishing, swore.

Ducks swam sideways
as the tipsy boat slipped past,
caught a spoke portside, shifted,
its rayon filling like a tub.

Minutes after takeoff, the umbrella
sank, slid under dark water.
Watchers groaned, as if
the loss were personal, or cosmic.

A little girl laughed.
In her storybook at home,
a red and white umbrella
woggles down, nodding left
and right, until it hits the muddy floor.
Schools of carp and catfish come
to scout this thick-stemmed flower.

The angler, red and fishless,
packed his tackle,
cursing at his empty creel.
Tonight no shade, no supper
for his backyard table.

Fishing

With thin thread she fishes
in a murky pond. She would lure
fragments of last night's dreams
to her paperclip hook, reel
from the deeps,
these shimmering bits, sift
them in the shallows, stitch
them together, pull them
like silk scarves
through her sleeve until
a reconstructed fish appeared.
Then she could say: *The scales*
represent…the fins surely signify…
I will free this fish…I will cook it…
or *I never eat fish because*
of the little bones…

Power

"There she blows!" the captain calls out
from the bridge, as the whale blows
like a horse impatient in its stall.
When the humpback arches, we await
the dive: raised tail stock, flukes
slide under water with olympic grace.

The water in the wake grows circular
and still. "The whale's footprint,"
someone says, and we are silenced by
the sight until the humpback breaches:
one backward somersault, pectoral fins
aflap like luffing sails, draws a gasp
from us, as over she goes again, jocund
as a child turning cartwheels on the lawn.

Midday, the motorboat speeds us miles
back to shore to climb a mountain
from whose crest the whales are captives
in the bellies of our minds, and the sea is
once more small enough to fit our eyes.

Feeders

Ignoring the sign which reads
DO NOT FEED THE BIRDS
a man in a black wool coat
and a white-shoed lady feed the geese—
soft Blue Ribbon sandwich slices
from the market near the pond.

Two children, attentive as dogs, watch
until the old man shares his store
with them. One boy, no bigger than
the eager geese, retreats two steps
for every one the geese advance.
Tearing bits of bread before him,
he backs up, finds he's out of food.
"Stop! No more! That's ALL!"
he pleads and waves his hands.

The first goose turns; the others
"tsk" like disapproving matrons, then
follow slowly where she leads:
back to the old man wearing wool
and the white-shoed lady
who is wife or nurse.

Aim

The hunter shoots the quail; they fall
to grasses. He retrieves them
with his gloved hand, stuffs them
in the game bag, his voice
instructing me that unshot birds
will starve. As if bullet-struck myself,
I stumble into memory's glaring light,
and see a grassy shore at home,
a duckling stoned by boys—
boys stunned by the sharpness of their aim.

Urgency of Birds

Blackbirds are flying hard
above the back lawn where I sit
reading *A Serious Way of Wondering*,
whose writer is convinced the ethics
of the risen Christ are those that count:
feed my sheep, tend my lambs.

The birds fly in masses, in waves
like soldiers at Antietam, though met
with no opposing force. The autumn air
is warm, the oaks are welcoming.
A few birds land in trees other than
the leaders', but soon surrender.
It's all or nothing. The air is loud
with birds, then silent. Urgently
they fly south to feed,
with no command to love each other,
only to follow, stay with the flock.

And God knows when one falls.

Cat Girl

My daughter's cat perches
on the rim of the toilet.
He leans towards the bowl,
and bats a brave paw
across its little pond.

◆

Once I watched a boy in a boat
toss his cat overboard, then curse
as the terrified cat clawed
its way back up his bare arm
onto the gunwale.

◆

At summer camp, the cold
lake water shocked me
like a daily death. Bloodless, I ran
to the changing shed, my red wool
tank suit sodden as fur.

◆

Mornings, when cold water
hits my face, I want to claw
my way up the bare arm
of day, crouch back down
into the old dry boat of night.

The Shirt

I slip my arms
into your shirt;
it smells of tinned
tobacco—the pipe
my father held
in his teeth—or
like pine planks
cut for kitchen
shelves, sweet
as new-mown grasses
sweating in the sun.

The flannel
of your shirt
is soft as skin
but safer to be in.
A man's world—
it drums in me,
shouts like horns,
clicks in my heels
like castanets.

Alice

"Alice C. Turnipseed,…81,…a self-taught florist…died Saturday."
— *obituary*, The Baltimore Sun

Even as a child, Alice loved flowers.
Her mother would find her sitting
cross-legged among clumps of daffodils,
comfortably quiet with them as if
belonging to their group. She loved fruits
and vegetables too, not to eat so much
as to view in the garden, or hold when harvested.
She admired the glossy skin of the eggplant—
its purple, and the pale kernels of corn
in their rows, the homely wrap of the potato,
the ruddy radish. When, at twenty, she met
Willis Turnipseed, she married him, with
a vague hope of bearing turnips—not just sons.

Apple Pie

*"The fear of mice is an anxiety
of our own murderousness,
because mice symbolize our weaknesses."*
— *Silverman*

Because of the homemade apple pie,
we had the cheese.
Because of the cheese or the winter sky,
we had the mouse.

Meeting a mouse upstairs
made me more murderous
than the farmer's wife who took only tails.

I took with a doorstop the entire life.

Now a member of the Humane Society,
murderer member,
my hair and skin gone gray,
I wait for the THUD. The doorstop, any day.

The Charm

The ruined road attracted us—
two girls too old for dolls, too young

for boys, cousins crossing summer miles
to meet at grandma's house. One day we dared

to hike the red dirt road
to Emmie Byceler's place,

a haunted house we'd heard about for years,
terrified we'd find her standing

by the broken door. We crept inside
and found a calendar hung cockeyed

on the wall. Each brittle page we turned
held large black Xes in the squares of days.

With fear and hope, we looked for bones and
smelled a smell we knew must be a corpse,

but all we found was evidence of mice
and mouldering magazines along a wall.

We guessed what furniture went where,
which room she used to chop off legs,

what she cooked and where she slept,
if she ever did live here—or anywhere.

Maybe Emmie, who grandma said
was "touched," had died—been murdered—here!

Before we left, we pledged we'd never tell a soul.
With sticks we lettered in the road's red clay:

Ann Van Antwerp Lane, our grandma's name, a claim
on this red road, a charm to keep the ghost at bay.

The Landlady

She watches from her window,
watches him parallel park, fix
the red club on the steering wheel,
gather his text books, mount
the front steps. She hears his boots
on the stairs to his attic room—
stairs she will mount to deliver his mail.

She will stand close enough to feel
the force of his frame, notice
his heavy boots and the dark denim
collapsed on them. She stands
at the window, imagining herself
young and slight enough
to be lifted by his arms. She thinks
of the small curves of his ear,
the stretch of his shoulders.

She would cook a soup for him.
He, pressing his back to the chair,
would say, "Delicious. Delicious."
She would return his inscrutable smile.
Then he would ask, "Are you cold?
Take my sweater—please."

For Better or for Worse

I am not
the same person
I once was. Not
at all. Small
yellow pills
balancing the brain's
supply of serotonin
slash through
the Gordian knots
my stomach knits: fears
of fatal illnesses,
fluorescent lights,
family snares—
gone—along with
my libido,
and its dangerous blue eyes.

Call and Answer

He's upstairs and frantic
for a mate: one wing scraping
on the other a song of love.
Males alone make music;
this one captures only me,
the woman of the house.
My desire is to help, to set
him singing out of doors,
but when I try
to talk him into yielding,
he retreats behind a heating pipe.
It seems he'd rather die
than take a chance
on me and my intentions.
He dies, of course,
as I may too, silently,
behind a heating pipe.

Truck

The front seat of his truck, full
of fast food flotsam, smells of gas
and cigarettes. The woods beyond

his windshield lure me too, disheveled
light and dark, like morning news
tossed on the dashboard's edge.

I'm tired of keeping spaces trim: beds
made, floors scrubbed, dishes put away—
I like this tangled wood, this life in disarray.

There Is a Green Hill Far Away

on which retired horses graze.
Across a newly tarmacked street, a blaze
of sun leaps from the razor wire to
the eye of an amazed observer who
squints to see the line of boys in suits—
prison suits, bright orange or navy blue.
The boys are marching to the asphalt court;
they'll throw some hoops and then report
to Main for "anger management." Behind
the Juvenile Facility, white pine
and oaks surround a practice shooting range
for the police. The guns exchange
their fire; the air explodes with noise;
the horses on the hill, the line of boys
don't seem to mind; they're all resigned
to this irregular neighborhood design.

Litany for the Sick and the Well

Hear us, Lord.

Bring forth on bare heads
bunches of wisteria.

Grow banks of cyclamen
where breasts are gone.

For knees and hips,
sapling boughs.

Hear us, Lord.

Open ears to songs of lilac;
let toes braid with grasses,

pores breathe electric air
from earth. Send ions up

the primrose spines,
the hollyhockal lumbars.

Let blind eyes, mudwashed,
see trees walk.

For failing hearts,
plum trees in bloom.

Hear us, Lord of Light.

Pageant

In Market Square Arena
a priest was elevated,
consecrated—BISHOP!
Brasses blew. Choirs
lunged at Bach. Young acolytes
in red and old brocaded
churchmen carrying crooks
paraded under banners—like last year's
Ringling's Circus, when
it came to Market Square, with twelve
trained polar bears kneeling
where the clergy knelt.
Dancing dogs pranced and bowed,
and parti-colored clowns,
on decorated ponies,
were elevated too!

Looking at a Gerbil

Wrested from the pet store's anonymity,
praised and petted generously,
christened privately,
set on a wheel to exercise aerobically,
free from predators to nestle softly
in one corner of the cage, excreting
in another after eating
pellets of well-balanced meals, taking
guided field trips across the bedroom or
the kitchen floor—
a gerbil's life seems to me
perfection in captivity.

Purple Coat

The first time she wore the coat,
one of its flat black buttons flew off

like an angry crow, exposing
her neck to the cold. Nevertheless,

she was bolder wearing that coat,
its pyretic purple startling the night.

After a few years, the entire flock
of buttons disappeared, even those

whose purpose was simply to perch
on sleeves. Still, eyes followed her,

their whites overcast with fuchsia.
Right now she is standing near

the window's light, licking an end
of thread, poking its little point

through a needle's eye. She is set
to tame this wild coat. But wait:

the purple sleeves begin to flap!
The woolly bulk of winter coat arises

from the window ledge,
while on a table where the spool

and scissors lie, a dozen
egg-shaped buttons start to roll.

You Go Girl

Going 70 on Route 60 West,
I hear a motorcycle revving up to pass.
The rider is a she: her bleached jeans
frayed and flapping, fringed cowboy boots
atilt, leather jacket tight
across her back. She keeps abreast of me,
riding the road fearlessly.
In my Ford Explorer I'm afraid of curves,
afraid this car could overturn;
but she's my dolphin, leading me, Magellan,
through the Straits, her flying hair
a signal to fling out the sails.

Rowing

I row in my little boat
on the sea which takes me
where it will—and still
I row.